PSEUDOMONARCHIA

DÆMONIUM

PSEUDOMONARCHIA

DÆMONIUM

JOHANN WEYER

PSEUDOMONARCHIA
DÆMONUM.

Johann Weyer

"O curas hominum, ô quantum est in rebus inane?"

-- C. Lucilius, Satires of Persius

LECTORIS.

Ne *Sathanicæ factionis monopolium usqueadeo porro delitescat, hanc Dæmonum Pseudomonarchiam, ex Acharonticorum Vasallorum archivo subtractam, in hujus Operis de Dæmonum præstigiis calce annectere volui, ut effascinatorum id genus hominum, qui se magos jactitare non erubescunt, curiositas, præstigiæ, vanitas, dolus, imposturæ, deliria, mens elusa, & manifesta mendacia, quinimo non ferendæ blasphemiæ, omnium mortalium, qui in mediæ lucis splendore hallucinari nolint, oculis clarissimè appareant, hoc potissimum seculo scelestissimo, quo Christi regnum tam enormi impunitaque tyrannide impetitur ab iis qui Beliali palàm sacramentum præstitêre, stipendium etiam justum hauddubie recepturi: quibus & perditas has horas libenter dedico, si forte ex immensa Dei misericordia convertantur & vivant: quod ex animo iis precor, sitque felix & faustum. Ne autem curiosulus aliquis, fascino nimis detentus, hoc stultitiæ argumentum temere imitari audeat, voces hinc inde prætermisi studio, ut universa delinquendi occasio præcideretur. Inscribitur vero à maleferiato hoc hominum genere Officium spirituum, vel, Liber officiorum spirituum, seu, Liber dictus Empto. Salomonis, de principibus & regibus dæmoniorum, qui cogi possunt divina virtute & humana. At mihi nuncupabitur Pseudomonarchia Dæmonum.*

PSEUDOMONARCHIA

DÆMONUM.

(1) Primus Rex, qui est de potestate Orientis, dicitur Baël, apparens tribus capitibus, quorum unum assimilatur bufoni alterum homini, tertium feli. Rauca loquitur voce, formator morum & insignis certator, reddit hominem invisibilem & sapientem. Huic obediunt sexagintasex legiones.

(2) Agares Dux primus sub potestate Orientis, apparet benevolus in senioris hominis forma, equitans in crocodilo, & in manu accipitrem portans. Cuncta linguarum genera docet optime: fugitantes reverti facit, & permanentes fugere: prælaturas & dignitates dimittit, & tripudiare facit spiritus terræ: & est de ordine Virtutum, sub sua potestate habens triginta & unam legiones.

(3) Marbas, alias Barbas, Præses magnus, se manifestans in fortissimi leonis specie, sed ab exorcista accitus humana induitur forma, & de occultis plene respondet, morbos invehit & tollit, promovet sapientiam artiumque mechanicarum cognitionem, homines adhæc in aliam mutat formã. Præest trigintasex legionibus.

(4) Pruflas, alibi invenitur Bufas, magnus Princeps & Dux est, cujus mansio circa turrim Babylonis, & videtur in eo flamma foris, caput autem assimilatur magno nycticoraci. Autor est & promotor discordiarum, bellorum, rixarum & mendaciorum. Omnibus in locis non intromittatur. Ad quæsita respondet abunde. Sub sunt huic legiones vinginti sex, partim ex ordine Throni, partim Angelorum.

(5) Amon vel Aamon Marchio magnus & potens, prodit in lupi forma caudam habens serpentinam, & flammam evomens. Hominis autem indutus speciem, caninos ostentat dentes, & caput magno nycticoraci simile. Princeps omnium fortissimus est, intelligens præterita & futura, hinc & gratiam concilians omnium amicorum & inimicorum. Quadraginta imperat legionibus.

(6) Barbatos magnus Comes & Dux, apparet in signo Sagittarii silvestris cum quatuor regibus tubas ferentibus. Intelligit cantus avium, canum latratus, mugitus boum & cunctorum animalium: thesauros item à magis & incantatoribus reconditos, detegit: Et est ex ordine Virtutum, partim Dominationum. Triginta præsidet legionibus. Novit præterita & futura: tam amicorum quam inimicorum animos conciliat.

*(7) Buer Præses magnus conspicitur in signo *. Absolute docet philosophiam, practicam, ethica item & logica, & herbarum vires: Dat optimos familiares: Ægros sanitati restituere novit, maxime & homines. Quinquaginta legionum habet imperium.*

(8) Gusoyn Dux magnus & fortis, apparet in forma zenophali. Explicate respondet & vere de præsentibus, præteritis, futuris & occultis. Amicoram & inimicorum gratiam reddit: Dignitates confert & honores conformat. Præest quadragintaquinque legionibus.

(9) Botis, alibi Otis, magnus Præses & Comes, Prodit in viperæ specie deterrima: Et siquando formam induit humanam dentes ostendit magnos & cornua duo, manu gladium acutum portans. Dat perfecte responsa vera de præsentius, præteritis, futuris & abstrusis. Tam amicos quam hostes conciliat. Sexaginta imperat legionibus.

(10) Bathym, alibi Marthim Dux magnus & fortis: Visitur constitutione viri fortissimi cum cauda serpentina, equo pallido insidens. Virtutes herbarum & lapidum pretiosorum intelligit. Cursu velocissimo hominem de regione in regionem transfert. Huic triginta subsunt legiones.

(11) Pursan, alias Curson, magnus Rex, prodit ut homo facie leonina, viperam portans ferocissimam, ursoque insidens, quem semper præcedunt tubæ. Callet præsentia, præterita & futura: Aperit occulta, thesauros detegit: Corpus humanum suscipit & aëreum. Vere respondet de rebus terrenis & occultis, de divinitate & mundi creatione: Familiares parit optimos: Cui parent vigintiduo legiones, partim de ordine Virtutum, partim ex ordine Throni.

(12) Eligor, alias Abigor, Dux magnus,apparet ut miles pulcherrimus, lanceam, vexillum & sceptrum portans. Plene de occultis respondet atque bellis, & quomodo milites occurrere debeant: Futura scit, & gratiam apud omnes dominos & milites conciliat. Præsidet sexaginta legionibus.

(13) Loray, alias Oray, magnus Marchio, se ostendens in forma sagittarii pulcherrimi, pharetram & arcum gestantis: author existit omnium præliorum, & vulnera putrefacit quæ à sagittariis infliguntur, quos objicit optimos tribus diebus. Triginta dominatur legionibus.

(14) Valefar, alias Malaphar, Dux est fortis, forma leonis prodiens & capite latronis. Familiaritatem parit suis, donec laqueo suspendantur. Decem præsidet legionibus.

(15) Morax, alias Foraii, magnus Comes & Præses: Similis tauro visitur: Et si quando humanam faciem assumit, admirabilem in Astronomia & in omnibus artibus liberalibus reddit hominem: parit etiam famulos non malos

& sapientes: novit & herbarum & pretiosorum lapidum potentiam. Imperat triginta sex legionibus.

(16) Ipes, alias Ayperos est magnus Comes & Princeps, apparens quidem specie angelica, interim leone obscurior & turpis, capite leonis, pedibus anserinis, cauda leporina. Præterita & futura novit: Redditque hominem ingeniosum & audacem. Legiones huic obediunt trigintasex.

(17) Naberus, alias Cerberus, Marchio est fortis, forma corvi se ostentans: Si quando loquitur, raucam edit vocem. Reddit & hominem amabilem & artium intelligentem, cum primis in Rhetoricis eximium. Prælaturarum & dignitatum jacturam parit. Novendecim legiones hunc audiunt.

(18) Glasya labolas, alias Caacrinolaas vel Caassimolar magnus Præses: Qui progreditur ut canis habens alas gryphi. Artium cognitionem dat, interim dux omnium homicidarum. Præsentia & futura intelligit. Tam amicorum quam inimicorum animos demeretur: Et hominem reddit invisibilem. Imperium habet triginta sex legionum.

(19) Zepar Dux magnus, apparens uti miles, inflammansque virorum amore mulieres, & quando ipsi jussum fuerit, earum formam in aliam transmutat, donec dilectis suis fruantur. Steriles quoque eas facit. Vigintisex huic parent legiones.

(20) Byleth Rex magnus & terribilis, in equo pallido equitans, quem præcedunt tubæ, symphoniæ, & cuncta Musicæ genera. Quum autem coram exorcista se ostentat, turgidus ira & furore videtur, ut decipiat. Exorcista vero tum sibi prudenter caveat: Atque ut fastum ei adimat, in manu suscipiat baculum corili, cum quo orientem & meridiem versus, foris juxta circulum manum extendet, facietque triangulum. Cæterum si manum non extendit, &

intrare jubet, atque spirituum Vinculum ille renuerit, ad lectionem progrediatur exorcista: mox ingredietur item submissus, ibi stando & faciendo quodcunque jufferit exorcista ipsi Byleth regi, eritque securus. Si vero contumacior fuerit, nec primo jussu circulum ingredi voluerit, reddetur forte timidior exorcista: Vel si Vinculum spirituum minus habuerit, sciet haud dubie exorcista, malignos spiritus postea eum non verituros, at semper viliorem habituros. Item si ineptior sit locus triangulo deducendo juxta circulum, tunc vas vino plenum ponatur: Et intelliget exorcista certissimè, quum è domo sua egressus fuerit cum sociis suis, prædictum Byleth sibi fautorem fore, benevolum, & coram ipso submissum quando progredietur. Venientem vero exorcista benigne suscipiat, & de ipsius fastu glorietur: Propterea quoque eundem adorabit, quemadmodum alii reges, quia nihil dicit absque aliis principibus. Item si hic Byleth accitus fuerit ab aliquo exorcista, semper tenendus ad exorcistæ faciem annulus argenteus medii digiti manus sinistræ, quemadmodum pro Amaymone. Nec est prætermittenda dominatio & potestas tanti principis, quoniam nullus est sub potestate & dominatione exorcistæ alius, qui viros & mulieres in delirio detinet, donec exorcistæ voluntatem explerint: Et fuit ex ordine Potestatum, sperans se ad septimum Thronum rediturum, quod minus credibile. Imperat octogintaquinque legionibus.

(21) Sytry, alias Bitru, magnus Princeps, leopardi facie apparens, habensque alas velut gryphi. Quando autem humanam assumit formam, mire pulcher videtur. Incendit virum mulieris amore, mulierem vicissim alterius desiderio incitat. Jussus secreta libenter detegit feminarum, eas ridens ludificansque, ut se luxuriose nudent. Huic sexaginta legiones obsequuntur.

(22) Paymon obedit magis Lucifero quam alii reges.
Lucifer hic intelligendus, qui in profunditate scientiæ suæ
demersus, Deo assimilari voluit, & ob hanc arrogantiam in
exitium projectus est. De quo dictum est: Omnis lapis
pretiosus operimentum tuum Ezech. 28 . Paymon autem
cogitur virtute divina, ut se sistat coram exorcista: ubi
hominis induit simulachrum, insidens dromedario,
coronaque insignitus lucidissima, & vultu fœmineo. Hunc
præcedit exercitus cum tubis & cimbalis bene sonantibus,
atque omnibus instrumentis Musicis, primo cum ingenti
clamore & rugitu apparens, sicut in Empto. Salomonis, &
arte declaratur. Et si Paymon hic quandoque loquitur, ut
minus ab exorcista intelligatur, propterea is non tepescat:
sed ubi porrexerit illi primam chartam ut voto suo
obsequatur, jubebit quoque ut distincte & aperte
respondeat ad quæsita, & de universa philosophia &
prudentia vel scientia, & de cæteris arcanis. Et si voles
cognoscere dispositionem mundi, & qualis sit terra, aut
quid eam fustineat in aqua, aut aliquid aliud, & quid sit
abyssus, & ubi est ventus & unde veniat, abunde te docebit.
Accedant & consecrationes tam de libationibus quam aliis.
Confert hic dignitates & confirmationes. Resistentes sibi
suo vinculo deprimit, & exorcistæ subjicit. Bonos comparat
famulos, & artium omnium intellectum. Notandum, quod in
advocando hunc Paymonem, Aquilonem versus exorcistam
conspicere oporteat, quæ ibi hujus sit hospitium. Accitum
vero intrepide constanterque suscipiat, interroget, & ab eo
petat quicquid voluerit, nec dubie impetrabit. At ne
creatorem oblivioni tradat, cavendum exorcistæ, propter ea
quæ præmissa fuerunt de Paymone. Sunt qui dicunt, eum ex
ordine Dominationum fuisse: sed aliis placet, ex ordine
Cherubin. Hunc sequuntur legiones ducentæ, partim ex
ordine Angelorum, partim Potestatum. Notandum adhæc, si
Paymon solus fuerit citatus per aliquam libationem aut
sacrificium, duo reges magni comitantur, scilicet Bebal &
Abalam, & alii potentes. In hujus exercitu sunt

13

vigintiquinque legiones: Quia spiritus his subjecti, non semper ipsis adsunt, nisi ut appareant, divina virtute compellantur.

(23) Regem Belial aliqui dicunt statim post Luciferum fuisse creatum, ideoque sentiunt ipsum esse patrem & seductorem eorum qui ex Ordine ceciderunt. Cecidit enim prius inter alios digniores & sapientiores, qui præcedebant Michaëlem & alios cœlestes angelos, qui decrant. Quamvis autem Belial ipsos qui in terram dejecti fuerint, præcesserit: alios tamen qui in cœlo mansere, non antecessit. Cogitur hic divina virtute, cum accipit sacrificia, munera & holocausta, ut vicissim det immolantibus responsa vera: At per horam in veritate non perdurat, nisi potentia divina compellatur, ut dictum est. Angelicam assumit imagine in impense pulchram, in igneo curru sedens. Blande loquitur. Tribuit dignitates & prælaturas senatorias, gratiam item amicorum, & optimos famulos. Imperium habet octoginta legionum, ex ordine partim Virtutum, partim Angelorum. Forma exorcistæ invenitur in Vinculo Spirituum. Observandum exorcistæ, hunc Belial in omnibus succurrere suis subditis: Si autem se submittere noluerit, Vinculum Spirituum legatur, quo sapientissimus Salomon eos cum suis legionibus in vase vitreo relegavit: Et relegati cum omnibus legionibus fuere septuagintaduo reges, quorum primus erat Bileth, secundus Belial, deinde Asmoday, & circirer mille millia legionum. Illud proculdubio à magistro Salomone didiciste me fateor: Sed causam relegationis me non docuit, crediderim tamen propter arrogantiam ipsius Belial. Sunt quidam necromantici, qui asserunt, ipsum Salomonem quodam die astutia cujusdam mulieris seductum, orando se inclinasse versus simulacrum Belial nomine. Quod tamen fidem non meretur: Sed potius sentiendum, ut dictum est, propter superbiam & arrogantiam, relegatos esse in magno vase, projectos in Babylone in puteum grandem valde. Enimvero

prudentissimus Salomon divina potentia suas exequebatur operationes, quæ etiam nunquam eum destituit: propterea simulachrum non adorasse ipsum sentiendum est, alioqui divina virtute spiritus cogere nequivisset. Hic autem Belial cum tribus regibus in puteo fuit. At Babylonienses ad hæc exhorrescentes, rati se thesaurum amplum in puteo inventuros, unanimi consilio in puteum descenderunt, detegeruntque & confregere vas, unde mox egressi captivi, in proprium locum porto sunt rejecti. Belial vero ingressus quoddam simulachrum, dabat responsa sibi immolantibus & sacrificantibus, ut testatur Tocz in dictis suis: Et Babylonienses adorantes sacrificaverunt eidem.

(24) Bune Dux magnus & fortis, apparet ut draco, tribus capitibus, tertium vero assimilatur homini. Muta loquitur voce: Mortuos locum mutare facit, & dæmones supra defunctorum sepulchra congregari: omnimodo hominem locupletat, redditque loquacem & sapientem: ad quæsita vere respondet. Huic legiones parent triginta.

(25) Forneus magnus Marchio, similis monstro marino, reddit hominem in Rhetoricis admirabilem, optima fama & linguarum peritia ornat, tam amicis quam inimicis gratum facit. Subsunt huic vigintinovem legiones, ex ordine partim Thronorum, partim Angelorum.

(26) Roneve Marchio & Comes, assimilatur monstro. Singularem in Rhetoricis intelligcntiam confert, famulos item fidos, linguarum cognitionem, amicorum & inimicorum favorem. Huic obediunt legiones novendecim.

(27) Berith Dux magnus & terribilis: tribus nuncupatur nominibus, à quibusdam Beal, à Judæis Berith, à necromanticis Bolfri. Prodit ut miles ruber cum vestitu rubro, & equo ejusdem coloris coronaque ornatus. Vere de

15

præsentibus, præteritis & futuris respondet. Virtute divina per annulum magicæ artis ad horam scilicet cogitur. Mendax etiam est. In aurum cuncta metallorum genera mutat. Dignitatibus ornat easdemque confirmat: Claram subtilemque edit vocem. Viginti sex legiones huic subsunt.

(28) Astaroth Dux magnus & fortis, prodiens angelica specie turpissima, insidensque in dracone infernali, & viperam portans manu dextra. Vere respondet de præteritis, præsentibus, futuris & occultis. Libenter de spirituum creatore, & eorundem lapsu loquitur, quomodo peccaverint & ceciderint. Se spontè non prolapsum esse dicit. Reddit hominem mire eruditum in artibus liberalibus. Quadraginta legionibus imperat. Ab hoc quilibet exocista caveat, ne prope nimis cum admittat, ob fœtorem intolerabilem quem expirat. Itaque annulum argenteum magicum in manu sua juxta faciem teneat, quo se ab injuria facile tuebitur.

(29) Forras vel Forcas magnus Præses est: visitur forma viri fortissimi, & in humana specie vires herbarum & lapidum preciosorum intelligit. Plene docet Logica, Ethica & corundem partes. Reddit hominem invisibilem, ingeniosum, loquacem & vivacem: Amissa recuperat, thesauros detegit. Dominium viginti novem legionum habet.

(30) Furfur Comes est magnus, apparens ut cervus cauda flammea. In omnibus mentitur, nisi in triangulum intro ducatur. Jussus angelicam assumit imaginem. Rauca loquitur voce: amorem inter virum & mulierem libenter conciliat: novit & concitare fulgura, coruscationes & tonitrua in iis partibus ubi jussum fuerit. De occultis & divinis rebus bene respondet. Imperat legionibus vigintisex.

(31) Marchocias magnus Marchio est. Se ostentat specie lupæ ferocissimæ cum alis gryphi, cauda serpentina, & ex ore nescio quid evomens. Quum hominis imaginem induit,

pugnator est optimus. Ad quæsita vere respondet: fidelis in cunctis exorcistæ mandatis. Fuit ordinis Dominationum. Huic subjacent legiones triginta. Sperat se post mille ducentos annos ad septimum Thronum reversurum: sed ea spe falsus est.

(32) Malphas magnus Præses, conspicitur corvo similis: sed hominis idolum indutus rauca fatur voce. Domos & turres ingentes mire extruit, & obvios cito facit artifices maximos: Hostium vero ædes & turres dejicit. Famulos suppeditat non malos. Sacrificia libenter suscipit, at sacrificatores omnes fallit. Quadraginta huic parent legiones.

(33) Vepar, alias Separ, Dux magnus & fortis: Similis syreni: Ductor est aquarum & navium armis onustarum. Ut mare jussu magistri turgidum navibusque plenum appareat, efficit: contra inimicos exorcistæ per dies tres vulneribus putrescentibus vermesque producentibus homines inficit, à quibus tamen negotio absoluto sanantur omnes. Imperat legionibus vigintinovem.

(34) Sabnac, alias Salmac, Marchio magnus & fortis: prodit ut miles armatus, capite leonis, in pallido equo infidens. Hominis formam transmutat mire: Turres magnas armis plenas ædificat, item castra & civitates. Triginta dies ex mandato exorcistæ homini vulnera putrida & verminantia infligit. Familiares conciliat bonos: dominium exercens quinquaginta legionum.

(35) Sydonay, alias Asmoday, Rex magnus, fortis & potens: Visitur tribus capitibus, quorum primum assimilatur capiti tauri, alterum hominis, tertium arietis. Cauda ejus serpentina, ex ore flammam eructat, pedes anserini. Super dracone infernali sedet, in manu lanceam & vexillum portans. Præcedit alios qui sub potestate Amaymonis sunt.

17

Cum hujus officia exercet exorcista, fit fortis, cautus & in pedibus stans: si vero coopertus fuerit, ut in omnibus detegatur, efficiet: Quod si non fecerit exorcista, ab Amaymone in cunctis decipietur: Sed mox cum ipsum in prædicta forma conspicit, appellabit illum nomine suo, inquiens: Tu vero es Asmoday. Ipse non negabit: Et mox ad terram. Dat annulum virtutum: Docet absolute Geometriam, Arithmeticam, Astronomiam, Mechanicam: Ad interrogata plene & vere respondet: Hominem reddit invisibilem: Loca thesaurorum ostendit & custodit, si fuerit de legionibus Amaymonis. In sua potestate legiones septuaginta duas habet.

(36) Gaap, alias Tap, Præses magnus & Princeps: in signo Meridiei apparet: sed quum humanam assumit faciem Clm 849, fol 66r: Apparet in signo medici cum suscipit figuram humanam; est doctor opti m us mulierum, et facit ardere in amorem virorum , ductor est præcipuorum quatuor regum, tam potens ut Byleth. Extiterunt autem quidam necromantici, qui huic libamina & holocausta obtulere, & ut eundem evocarent, artem exercuere, dicentes sapientissimum Salomonem eam composuisse, quod falsum est: imo fuit Cham filius Noë, qui primus post diluvium cœpit malignos invocare spiritus, invocavit autem Byleth, & composuit artem in suo nomine, & librum, qui multis mathematicis est cognitus. Fiebant autem holocausta, libamina, munera, & multa nefaria, quæ operabantur exorcistæ admistis sanctissimis Dei nominibus, quæ in eadem arte sparsim exprimuntur. Epistola vero de iis nominibus est conscripta à Salomone, uti & scribunt Helias Hierosolymitanus & Heliseus. Notandum, si aliquis exorcista habuerit artem Beleth, nec ipsum coram se sistere possit aut videre, nisi per artem: Quomodo autem eundem continere oporteat, non est explicandum, quum sit nefandum, & nihil à Salomone de ejus dignitate & officio didicerim, hoc tamen non silebo, ipsum reddere hominem

admirabilem in philosophia & artibus omnibus liberalibus. Facit ad amorem, odium, invisibilitatem & consecrationem eorum quæ sunt de dominatione Amaymonis: Et de potestate alterius exorcistæ tradit familiares, & vera perfecte responsa de præsentibus, præteritis & futuris. Velocissimo transcursu in varias regiones traducit hominem. Sexagintasex præest legionibus, & fuit de Potestatum ordine.

(37) Chax, alias Scox, Dux est & Marchio magnus: Similis ciconiæ rauca voce & subtili. Mirabiliter aufert visum, auditum & intellectum jussu exorcistæ: aufert pecuniam ex qualibet domo regia, & reportat post mille ducentos annos, si jussus fuerit: abripit & equos. Fidelis esse in omnibus mandatis putatur: ac licet se obsecuturum exorcistæ promittat, non tamen in omnibus facit. Mendax est, nisi in triangulum introducatur: introductus autem loquitur de rebus divinis & reconditis thesauris, qui à malignis spiritibus non custodiuntur. Promittit insuper se collaturum optimos famulos, qui accepti sunt, si non fuerint deceptores. Huic subjacent legiones triginta.

(38) Pucel Dux magnus & fortis, apparet in specie angelica, sed obscura valde: loquitur de occultis: docet Geometriam & omnes artes liberales: sonitus facit ingentes, & sonare aquas ubi non sunt, easdem & calefacit & harum balnea recuperandæ sanitati servientia certis temporibus, distemperat jussu exorcistæ. Fuit de ordine Potestatum, habetque in sua potestate legiones quadragintaocto.

(39) Furcas miles est: prodit similitudine sævi hominis cum longa barba, & capillitio cano. In equo pallido insidet, portans in manu telum acutum. Docet perfecte practicam, philosophiam, rhetoricam, logicam, chiromantiam, astronomiam, piromantiam, & earum partes. Huic parent viginti legiones.

(40) Murmur magnus Dux & Comes: Apparet militis forma, equitans in vulture, & ducali corona comptus. Hunc præcedunt duo ministri tubis magnis: Philosophiam absolute docet. Cogit animas coram exorcista apparere, ut interrogatæ respondeant ad ipsius quæsita. Fuit de ordine partim Thronorum, partim Angelorum.

(41) Caym magnus Præses, formam assumens merulæ: at quum hominem induit, respondet in favilla ardente, ferens in manu glagium sic gladium acutissimum. Præ cæteris sapienter argumentari facit: Tribuit intellectum omnium volatilium, mugitus boum, latratus canum, & sonitus aquarum: de futuris optime respondet. Fuit ex ordine Angelorum. Præsidet legionibus triginta.

(42) Raum vel Raym Comes est magnus: Ut corvus visitur: Sed cum assumit humanam faciem, si ab exorcista jussus fuerit, mirè ex regis domo vel alia suffuratur, & ad locum sibi designatum transfert. Civitates destruit: Dignitatum despectum ingerit. Novit præsentia, præterita & futura. Favorem tam hostium quam amicorum conciliat. Fuit ex ordine Thronorum. Præest legionibus triginta.

(43) Halphas Comes magnus, prodit similis ciconiæ rauca voce. Insigniter ædificat oppida ampla armis plena: Bellum movet, & jussus, homines bellicosos ad designatum locum mittit obviam. Subsunt huic viginti sex legiones.

(44) Focalor Dux magnus, prodit velut homo, habens alas gryphi forma. Accepta humana figura, interficit homines & in aquis submergit. Imperat mari & vento, navesque bellicas subvertit. Notandum omni exorcistæ, si huic mandetur, ne homines lædat, libenter obsequitur. Sperat se post mille annos reversurum ad septimum Thronum, sed fallitur. Triginta legionibus imperat.

(45) Vine magnus Rex & Comes: se ostentat ut leo in equo nigro insidens, portansque viperam in manu. Amplas turres libenter ædificat: Lapideas domus extruit, rivos reddit turgidos: Ad exorcistæ mandatum respondet de occultis, maleficis, præsentibus, præteritis & futuris.

(46)Bifrons, monstri similitudine conspicitur. Ubi humanam assumit imaginem, reddit hominem in Astrologia mirabilem, planetarum mansiones absolute docens, idem præstat in Geometria, & mensuris aliis. Vires herbarum, lapidum pretiosorum & lignorum intelligit. Corpora mortuorum de loco ad locum transmutat: Candelas super defunctorum sepulchra inflammare videtur. Huic subjacent vinginti sex legiones.

(47) Gamygyn magnus Marchio: in forma equi parvi visitur: at ubi hominis simulachrum assumit, raucam edit vocem, de omnibus artibus liberalibus differens: efficit quoque, ut coram exorcista conveniant animæ in mari exeuntes, & quæ degunt in purgatorio (quod dicitur Cartagra, id est, afflictio animarum) & corpora aërea suscipiunt, apparentque evidenter, & ad interrogata respondent. Permanet apud exorcistam, donec ipsius votum expleverit. Triginta legiones in sua habet potestate.

(48) Zagam magnus Rex & Præses: ut taurus prodit cum alis ad modum gryphi: sed assumpta hominis forma, reddit hominem ingeniosum: transmutat cuncta metallorum genera in monetas illius ditionis, & aquam in vinum, & è diverso: sanguinem quoque in oleum, & contra: & stultum in sapientem. Præest triginta tribus legionibus.

(49) Orias Marchio magnus, visitur ut leo, in equo fortissimo equitans, cauda serpentina: in dextera portat duos grandes serpentes etiam exibilantes. Callet planetarum mansiones, & vires sidereas perfecte docet.

Transmutat homines: confert dignitates, prælaturas & confirmationes: Item amicorum & hostium favorem. Præsidet legionibus triginta.

(50) Volac magnus Præses: progreditur uti puer alis angeli, super dracone equitans duobus capitibus. De occultis thesauris perfecte respondet, & ubi serpentes videantur, quos & viribus dedestitutos tradit in exorcistæ manus. Dominium habet legionum triginta.

(51) Gomory Dux fortis & potens: apparet ut mulier pulcherrima: ac ducali cingitur corona, in camelo equitans. Bene & vere respondet de præteritis, præsentibus, futuris, & occultis thesauris ubi lateant. Conciliat amorem mulierum, & maxime puellarum. Imperat legionibus vigintisex.

(52) Decarabia vel Carabia, magnus Rex & Comes: venit similis *. Vires herbarum & lapidum pretiosorum novit: efficit ut aves coram exorcista volent, & velut familiares ac domesticæ morentur, bibant & cantillent suo more. Parent huic triginta legiones.

(53) Amduscias Dux magnus & fortis: procedit ut unicornu: in humana similiter forma, quando coram magistro suo se fistit: Et si præcipiatur, efficit facile ut tubæ & symphoniæ omniaque musicorum instrumentorum genera audiantur, nec tamen conspectui appareant: ut item arbores ad exorcistæ genu se inclinent. Optimus est una cum famulis. Imperium habet vigintinovem legionum.

(54) Andras magnus Marchio: visitur forma angelica, capite nycticoraci nigro simili, in lupo nigro & fortissimo equitans, bajulansque manu gladium acutissimum. Novit interficere dominum, servum & coadjutores: author est discordiarum. Dominatur legionibus triginta.

(55) Androalphus Marchio magnus, apparens ut pavo: graves edit sonitus: Et in humana forma docet perfecte geometriam & mensuram spectantia: reddit hominem in argumentando argutum, & in astronomia prudentem, eundemque in avis speciem transmutat. Triginta huic subsunt legiones.

(56) Oze Præses magnus, procedit similis leopardo: sed hominem mentitus, reddit prudentem in artibus liberalibus: vere resondet de divinis & occultis: transmutat hominis formam: & ad eam insaniam eum redigit, ut sibi persuadeat esse quod non est, quemadmodum se esse regem vel papam, & coronam in capite gestare: duratque id regnum horam.

(57) Aym vel Haborym Dux magnus & fortis: progreditur tribus capitibus, primo serpenti, simili, altero homini duos * habenti, tertio felino. In vipera equitat, ingentem facem ardentem portans, cujus flamma succenditur castrum vel civitas. Omnibus modis ingeniosum reddit hominem: de abstrusis rebus vere respondet. Imperat legionibus vigintisex.

(58) Orobas magnus Princeps: procedit equo conformis: hominis autem indutus idoltum, de virtute divina loquitur: vera dat responsa de præteritis, præsentibus, futuris, de divinitate & creatione: neminem decipit, nec tentari sinit: confert prælaturas & dignitates, amicorum item & hostium favorem. Præsidet legionibus viginti.

(59) Vapula Dux magnus & fortis: conspicitur ut leo alis ad modum gryphi. Reddit hominem subtilem & mirabilem in artibus mechanicis, philosophia, & scientiis quæ in libris continentur. Præfectus est trigintasex legionum.

(60) Cimeries magnus Marchio & fortis: imperans in partibus Africanis: docet perfecte Grammaticam, Logicam & Rhetoricam. Thesauros detegit, & occulta aperit. Facit ut homo cursu celerrimo videatur transmutari in militem. Equitat in equo nigro & grandi. Legionibus viginti præest.

(61) Amy Præses magnus: apparet in flamma ignea: sed humana assumpta forma, reddit hominem admirabilem in astrologia & omnibus artibus liberalibus. Famulos suppetit optimos: thesauros à spiritibus custoditos ostendit. Præfecturam habet legionem triginta sex, ex ordine partim angelorum, partim potestatum. Sperat se post mille ducentos annos ad Thronum septimum reversurum, quod credibile non est.

(62) Flauros dux fortis: conspicitur forma leopardi & terribili. In humana specie vultum ostentat horrendum, & oculos flammeos. De præteritis, præsentibus & futuris plene & vere respondet. Si fuerit in triangulo, mentitut in cunctis, & fallit in aliis negotiis. Libenter loquitur de divinitate, mundi creatione & lapsu. Divina virtute cogitur, & omnes alii dæmones sive spiritus, ut omnes adversarios exorcistæ succendant & destruant. Et si virtute numinis ipsi imperatum fuerit, exorcistæ tentationem non permittit. Legiones viginti sub sua habet potestate.

(63) Balam Rex magnus & terribilis: prodit tribus capitibus, primo tauri, altero hominis, tertio arietis: cauda adhæc serpentina, oculis flammeis, equitans in urso fortissimo, & accipitrem in manu portans. Raucam edit vocem: perfectè responet de præteritis, præsentibus & futuris: reddit hominem & invisibilem & prudentem. Quadraginta legionibus præsidet, & fuit ex ordine dominationum.

(64) Alocer Dux magnus & fortis: procedit ut miles in equo vasto insidens: facies ejus leonina, rubicunda valde cum

oculis flammeis: graviter loquitur: hominem reddit admirabilem in astronomia & in omnibus artibus liberalibus: confert bonam familiam; Dominatur triginta sex legionibus.

(65) Zaleos magnus Comes: apparet ut miles pulcherrimus in crocodilo equitans, & ducali ornatus corona, pacificus, &c.

(66)Wal Dux magnus & fortis: conspicitur ut dromedarius magnus ac terribilis: at in humana forma linguam sonat Ægyptiacam graviter. Hic præ cæteris amorem maxime mulierum conciliat: inde novit præsentia, præterita & futura: confert & gratiam amicorum atque inimicorum. De ordine fuit potestatum. Trigintaseptem legiones gubernat.

(67) Haagenti magnus Præses: ut taurus videtur, habens alas gryphi: sed assumpta facie humana, reddit hominem ingeniosum in quibuslibet: cuncta metalla in aurum transmutat, aquam in vinum, & ediverso. Tot legionibus imperat, quot Zagan.

(68) Phœnix magnus Marchio: apparet uti avis phœnix puerili voce: sed antequam se sistit coram exorcista, cantus emittit dulcissimos: tunc autem cavendum exorcistæ cum suis sociis, ne suavitati cantus aures accommodent, sed ille mox huic jubeat humanam assumere speciem, tunc mire loquetur de cunctis scientiis admirandis. Poëta est optimus & obediens. Sperat se post mille ducentos annos ad septimum thronum rediturum. Viginti præest legionibus.

(69) Stolas magnus Princeps: prodit forma nycticoracis: coram exorcista hominis simulachrum suscipit, docetque absolutè astronomiam. Herbarum & lapidum pretiosorum vires intelligit. Vigintisex legiones huic subjacent.

Legio 6666.

Secretum secretorum tu operans sis secretus horum.

Observa horas in quibus quatuor reges, scilicet Amoymon rex Orientalis, Gorson rex Meridionalis, Zymymar rex Septentrionalis, Goap rex & princeps Occidentalis possunt constringi, à tertia hora usque ad meridiem, à nona hora usque ad vesperas.

Item Marchiones à nona usque ad completorium, vel à completorio usque ad finem diei.

Item Duces à prima usque ad meridiem: & observatur cœlum clarum.

Item Prœlati in aliqua hora diei.

Item Milites ab aurora usque ad ortum solis, vel à vesperis usque ad finem solis.

Item Prœses in aliqua hora diei non potest constringi, nisi rex cui paret, invocaretur, & nec in crepusculo noctis.

Item Comites omni hora diei, dum sunt in locis campestribus vel sylvestribus, quo homines non solent accedere, &c.

Citatio Prœdictorum spirituum.

Ubi quem volueris spiritum, hujus nomen & officium supra cognosces: inprimis autem ab omni pollutione, minimum tres vel quatuor dies mundus esto in prima citatione, sic & spiritus postea obsequentiores erunt: fac & circulum, &

26

voca spiritum cum multa intentione: primum vero annulum in manu contineto: inde hanc recitato benedictionem tuo nomine & socii, si præsto fuerit, & effectum tui instituti sortieris, nec detrimentum à spiritibus senties: imo tuæ animæ perditionem.

2. In nomine Domini nostri Jesu Christi ✙ patris & ✙ filii & ✙ spiritus sancti: sancta trinitas & inseparabilis unitas te invoco, ut sis mihi salus & defensio & protectio corporis & animæ meæ, & omnium rerum mearum. Per virtutem sanctæ crucis ✙ & per virtutem passionis tuæ deprecor te domine Jesu Christe, per merita beatissimæ Mariæ virginis & matris tuæ atque omnium sanctorum tuorum, ut mihi concedas gratiam & potestatem divinam super omnes malignos spiritus, ut quoscunque nominibus invocavero, statim ex omni parte conveniant, & voluntatem meam perfecte adimpleant, quod mihi nihil nocentes, neque timorem inferentes, sed potius obedientes & ministrantes, tua districte virtute præcipiente, mandata mea perficiant, Amen. Sanctus sanctus sanctus dominus Deus Sabaoth, qui venturus es judicare vivos & mortuos: tu qui es & primus & novissimus, Rex regum & dominus dominantium Joth Aglanabrath El abiel anathi Enathiel Amazin sedomel gayes tolima Elias ischiros athanatos ymas heli Messias, per hæc tua sancta nomina & per omnia alia invoco te & obsecro te domine Jesu Christe, per tuam nativitatem, per baptismum tuum, per passionem & crucem tuam, per ascensionem tuam, per adventum spiritus sancti paracliti, per amaritudinem animæ tuæ; quando exivit de corpore tuo, per quinque vulnera tua, per sanguinem & aquam, quæ exierant de corpore tuo, per virtutem tuam, per sacramentum quod dedisti discipulis tuis pridie quam passus fuisti: per sanctam trinitatem, per individuam vnitatem, per beatam Mariam matrem tuam, per angelos & archangelos, per prophetas & patriarchas, & per omnes sanctos tuos, & per omnia sacramenta quæ fiunt in honore tuo: adoro te & obsecro te, benedico tibi & rogo, ut acceptes orationes has & conjurationes & verba oris mei, quibus uti voluero. Peto Domine Iesu Christe: da mihi virtutem & potestatem tuam super omnes angelos tuos, qui de cœlo ejecti sunt ad decipiendum genus humanum, ad attrahendum eos, ad constringendum, ad ligandum eos pariter & solvendum: Et ad congregandum eos coram me, & ad præcipiendum eis ut omnia, quæ possunt, faciant, & verba mea vocemque meam nullo modo contemnant: sed mihi & dictis meis obediant, & me timeant, per humanitatem & misericordiam & gratiam tuam deprecor & peto te adonay amay hortan vigedora mytay hel suranat ysion ysyesy & per omnia nomina tua sancta, per omnes sanctos & sanctas tuas per angelos & archangelos, potestates, dominationes & virtutes, & per illud nomen per quod Salomon contringebat dæmones, & conclusit ipsos Elhroch eban her agle goth joth othie venoch nabrat, & per omnia sacra nomina quæ scripta sunt in hoc libro & per virtutem eorundem, quatenus me potentem facias congregare & constringere omnes tuos spiritus de cœlo depulsos, ut mihi veraciter de omnibus meis interrogatis, de quibus quæram, responsionem veracem tribuant, & omnibus meis mandatis illi satisfaciant sine læsione corporis & animæ meæ & omnium ad me pertinentium, per Dominum nostrum Jesum Christum filium tuum, qui tecum vivit & regnat in unitate spiritus sancti Deus per omnia secula.

3. O pater omnipotens, ô fili sapiens, ô spiritus sancte corda hominum illustrans, ô vos tres in personis, una vero deitas in substantia: qui Adam & Evæ in peccatis eorum pepercistis, & propter eorum peccata mortem subiisti tu fili turpissimam, in lignoque sanctæ crucis sustinuisti: ô misericordissime, quando ad tuam confugio misericordiam, & supplico modis omnibus quibus possum, per hæc nomina sancta tui filii, scilicet & , & per omnia alia sua nomina, *quatenus concedas mihi virtutem & potestatem tuam, ut valeam tuos spiritus qui de cœlo ejecti sunt, ante me citare, & ut ipsi mecum loquantur, & mandata mea perficiant statim & sine mora, cum eorum voluntate, sine omni læsione corporis, animœ & bonorum meorum, &c. Continua ut in libro * Annuli Salomonis continetur.*

4. O summa & œterna virtus Altissimi, qui te disponente his judicio vocatis * vaycheon stimulamaton ezphares tetragrammaton olyoram irion esytion existion eryona onela brasym noym messias sother emanuël sabaoth adonay, te adoro, te invoco, totius mentis viribus meis imploro, quatenus per te prœsentes orationes & consecrationes & conjurationes consecrentur videlicet, & ubicunque maligni spiritus in virtute tuorum nominum sunt vocati, & omni parte conveniant, & voluntatem mei exorcisatoris diligenter adimpleant, fiat fiat fiat, Amen.

.5. Hœc blasphema & execranda hujus mundi fœx & sentina pœnam in magos prophanos bene constitutam, pro scelerato mentis ausu jure meretur.

FINIS

Pseudomonarchia Dæmonium

Johann Weyer

Translation in Reginald Scot
The Discoverie of Witchcraft

(1584)

Johann Wier, Pseudomonarchia daemonum. Salomons
notes of conjuration

PSEUDOMONARCHIA
DÆMONUM.

Johann Weyer

"Ah, human cares! Ah, how much futility in the world!"

-- C. Lucilius, Satires of Persius

An inventarie of the names, shapes, powers, governement, and effects of divels and spirits, of their severall segniories and degrees: a strange discourse woorth the reading.

READER.

(1) Baell . Their first and principall king (which is of the power of the east) is called Baëll who when he is conjured up, appeareth with three heads; the first, like a tode; the second, like a man; the third, like a cat. He speaketh with a hoarse voice, he maketh a man go invisible and wise , he hath under his obedience and rule sixtie and six legions of divels.

(2) Agares. The first duke under the power of the east, is named Agares, he commeth up mildile i.e. he appears willingly in the likenes of a faire old man, riding upon a crocodile, and carrieng a hawke on his fist; hee teacheth presentlie all maner of toongs, he fetcheth backe all such as runne awaie, and maketh them runne that stand still; he overthroweth all dignities supernaturall and temporall, hee maketh earthquakes, lit. "and makes spirits of the earth dance" and is of the order of vertues, having under his regiment thirtie one legions.

(3) Marbas, alias Barbas is a great president, and appeareth in the forme of a mightie lion; but at the commandement of a conjuror commeth up in the likenes of a man, and answereth fullie as touching anie thing which is hidden or

secret: he bringeth diseases, and cureth them, he promoteth wisedome, and the knowledge of mechanicall arts, or handicrafts; he changeth men into other shapes, and under his presidencie or gouvernement are thirtie six legions of divels conteined.

(4) Pruflas, otherwise found as Bufas, is a great prince and duke, whose abode is around the Tower of Babylon, and there he is seen like a flame outside. His head however is like that of a great night hawk. He is the author and promoter of discord, war, quarrels, and falsehood. He may not be admitted into every place. He responds generously to your requests. Under him are twenty-six legions, partly of the order of Thrones, and partly of the order of Angels.

(5) Amon, or Aamon, is a great and mightie marques, and commeth abroad in the likenes of a woolfe, having a serpents taile, spetting out and breathing vomiting flames of fier; when he putteth on the shape of a man, he sheweth out dogs teeth, and a great head like to a mightie raven night hawk ; he is the strongest prince of all other, and understandeth of all things past and to come, he procureth favor, and reconcileth both freends and foes, and ruleth fourtie legions of divels.

(6) Barbatos, a great countie or earle, and also a duke, he appeareth in Signo sagittarii sylvestris, with foure kings, which bring companies and great troopes. He understandeth the singing of birds, the barking of dogs, the lowings of bullocks, and the voice of all living creatures. He detecteth treasures hidden by magicians and inchanters, and is of the order of vertues, which in part beare rule: he knoweth all things past, and to come, and reconcileth freends and powers; and governeth thirtie legions of divels by his authoritie.

(7) Buer is a great president, and is seene in this signe * ;
he absolutelie teacheth philosophie morall and naturall, and
also logicke, and the vertue of herbes: he giveth the best
familiars, he can heale all diseases, speciallie of men, and
reigneth over fiftie legions.

(8) Gusoin Gusoyn is a great duke, and a strong,
appearing in the forme of a Xenophilus, he answereth all
things, present, past, and to come, expounding all questions.
He reconcileth freendship, and distributeth honours and
dignities, and ruleth over fourtie and five legions of divels.

(9) Botis, otherwise Otis, a great president and an earle he
commeth foorth in the shape of an ouglie lit. 'worst' viper,
and if he put on humane shape, he sheweth great teeth, and
two hornes, carrieng a sharpe sword in his hand: he giveth
answers of things present, past, and to come, and
reconcileth friends, and foes, ruling sixtie legions.

(10) Bathin Bathym , sometimes called Mathim Marthim ,
a great duke and a strong, he is seene in the shape of a verie
strong man, with a serpents taile, sitting on a pale horsse,
understanding the vertues of hearbs and pretious stones,
transferring men suddenlie from countrie to countrie, and
ruleth thirtie legions of divels.

(11) Purson Pursan , alias Curson, a great king, he
commeth foorth like a man with a lions face, carrieng a
most cruell viper, and riding on a beare; and before him go
alwaies trumpets, he knoweth things hidden, and can tell
all things present, past, and to come: he discloses hidden
things, he bewraieth treasure, he can take a bodie either
humane or aierie; he answereth truelie of all things earthlie
and secret, of the divinitie and creation of the world, and
bringeth foorth the best familiars; and there obeie him two

and twentie legions of divels, partlie of the order of vertues, & partlie of the order of thrones.

(12) Eligor, alias Abigor, is a great duke, and appeereth as a goodlie handsome knight, carrieng a lance, an ensigne, and a scepter: he answereth fullie of things hidden, and of warres, and how souldiers should meete: he knoweth things to come, and procureth the favour of lords and knights, governing sixtie legions of divels.

(13) Leraie Loray , alias Oray, a great marquesse, shewing himselfe in the likenesse of a galant handsome archer, carrieng a bowe and a quiver, he is author of all battels, he dooth putrifie all such wounds as are made with arrowes by archers, Quos optimos objicit tribus diebus, who best drives away mobs from the days (?) and he hath regiment over thirtie legions.

(14) Valefar, alias Malephar Malaphar , is a strong duke, comming foorth in the shape of a lion, and the head of a theefe or "barking" , he is verie familiar with them to whom he maketh himself acquainted, till he hath brought them to the gallowes, and ruleth ten legions.

(15) Morax, alias Foraii, a great earle and a president, he is seene like a bull, and if he take unto him a mans face, he maketh men wonderfull cunning in astronomie, & in all the liberall sciences: he giveth good familiars and wise, knowing the power & vertue of hearbs and stones which are pretious, and ruleth thirtie six legions.

(16) Ipos Ipes , alias Ayporos Ayperos , is a great earle and a prince, appeering in the shape of an angell, and yet indeed more obscure and filthie than a lion, with a lions head, a gooses feet, and a hares taile: he knoweth things to

come and past, he maketh a man wittie, and bold, and hath under his jurisdiction thirtie six legions.

(17) Naberius Naberus , alias Cerberus, is a valiant marquesse, shewing himselfe in the forme of a crowe, when he speaketh with a hoarse voice: he maketh a man amiable and cunning in all arts, and speciallie in rhetorike, he procureth the losse of prelacies and dignities: nineteene legions heare and obeie him.

(18) Glasya Labolas, alias Caacrinolaas, or Caassimolar, is a great president, who commeth foorth like a dog, and hath wings like a griffen, he giveth the knowledge of arts, and is the captaine of all mansleiers: he understandeth things present and to come, he gaineth the minds and love of freends and foes, he maketh a man go invisible, and hath the rule of six and thirtie legions.

(19) Zepar is a great duke, appearing as a souldier, inflaming women with the loove of men, and when he is bidden he changeth their shape, untill they maie enjoie their beloved, he also maketh them barren, and six and twentie legions are at his obeie and commandement.

(20) Bileth Byleth is a great king and a terrible, riding on a pale horsse, before whome go trumpets, and all kind of melodious musicke. When he is called up by an exorcist, he appeareth rough turgid and furious, to deceive him. Then let the exorcist or conjuror take heed to himself; and to allaje his courage, let him hold a hazell bat rod, staff, or stick in his hand, wherewithall he must reach out toward the east and south, and make a triangle without besides the circle; but if he hold not out his hand unto him, and he bid him come in, and he still refuse the bond or chain of spirits; let the conjuror proceed to reading, and by and by he will submit himselfe, and come in, and doo whatsoever the

exorcist commandeth him, and he shalbe safe. If Bileth the king be more stubborne, and refuse to enter into the circle at the first call, and the conjuror shew himselfe fearfull, or if he have not the chaine of spirits, certeinelie he will never feare nor regard him after. Also, if the place be unapt for a triangle to be made without the circle, then set there a boll of wine, and the exorcist shall certeinlie knowe when he commeth out of his house, with his fellowes, and that the foresaid Bileth will be his helper, his friend, and obedient unto him when he commeth foorth. And when he commeth, let the exorcist receive him courteouslie, and glorifie him in his pride, and therfore he shall adore him as other kings doo, bicause he saith nothing without other princes. Also, if he be cited by an exorcist, alwaies a silver ring of the middle finger of the left hand must be held against the exorcists face, as they doo for Amaimon. And the dominion and power of so great a prince is not to be pretermitted; for there is none under the power & dominion of the conjuror, but he that deteineth both men and women in doting better: "foolish" or "silly" love, till the exorcist hath had his pleasure. He is of the orders of powers, hoping to returne to the seaventh throne, which is not altogether credible, and he ruleth eightie five legions.

(21) Sitri Sytry , alias Bitru, is a great prince, appeering with the face of a leopard, and having wings as a griffen: when he taketh humane shape, he is verie beautiful, he inflameth a man with a womans love, and also stirreth up women to love men, being commanded he willinglie deteineth discloses secrets of women, laughing at them and mocking them, to make them luxuriouslie naked, and there obeie him sixtie legions.

(22) Paimon is more obedient in Lucifer than other kings are. Lucifer is heere to be understood he that was drowned in the depth of his knowledge: he would needs be like God,

and for his arrogancie was throwne out into destruction, of whome it is said; Everie pretious stone is thy covering (Ezech. 88 28.13 .). Paimon is constrained by divine vertue to stand before the exorcist; where he putteth on the likenesse of a man: he sitteth on a beast called a dromedarie, which is a swift runner, and weareth a glorious crowne, and hath an effeminate countenance. There goeth before him an host of men with trumpets and well sounding cymbals, and all musicall instruments. At the first he appeereth with a great crie and roring, as in Circulo Empto. Salomonis, and in the art is declared. And if this Paimon speake sometime that the conjuror understand him not, let him not therefore be dismaied. But when he hath delivered him the first obligation to observe his desire, he must bid him also answer him distinctlie and plainelie to the questions he shall aske you, of all philosophie, wisedome, and science, and of all other secret things. And if you will knowe the disposition of the world, and what the earth is, or what holdeth it up in the water, or any other thing, or what is Abyssus, or where the wind is, or from whence it commeth, he will teach you aboundantlie. Consecrations also as well of sacrifices offerings, libations as otherwise may be reckoned. He giveth dignities and confirmations; he bindeth them that resist him in his owne chaines, and subjecteth them to the conjuror; he prepareth good familiars, and hath the understanding of all arts. Note, that at the calling up of him, the exorcist must looke towards the northwest, bicause there is his house. When he is called up, let the exorcist receive him constantlie without feare, let him aske what questions or demands he list, and no doubt he shall obteine the same of him. And the exorcist must beware he forget not the creator, for those things, which have beene rehearsed before of Paimon, some saie he is of the order of dominations; others saie, of the order of cherubim. There follow him two hundred legions, partlie of the order of angels, and partlie of potestates. Note that if Paimon be cited alone by an offering or sacrifice, two kings followe him; to wit, Beball & Abalam, & other potentates: in his host are twentie five legions, bicause the spirits subject to them are not alwaies with them, except they be compelled to appeere by divine vertue.

(23) Some saie that the king Beliall was created immediatlie after Lucifer, and therefore they thinke that he was father and seducer of them which fell being of the orders. For he fell first among the worthier and wiser sort, which went before Michael and other heavenlie angels, which were lacking. Although Beliall went before all them that were throwne downe to the earth, yet he went not before them that tarried in heaven. This Beliall is constrained by divine venue, when he taketh sacrifices, gifts, and burnt offerings, that he againe may give unto the offerers true answers. But he tarrieth not one houre in the truth, except he be constrained by the divine power, as is said. He taketh the forme of a beautifull angell, sitting in a firie chariot; he speaketh faire, he distributeth preferments of senatorship, and the favour of friends, and excellent familiars: he hath rule over eightie legions, partlie of the order of vertues, partlie of angels; he is found in the forme of an exorcist in the bonds of spirits. The exorcist must consider, that this Beliall doth in everie thing assist his subjects. If he will not submit himselfe, let the bond of spirits be read: the spirits chaine is sent for him, wherewith wise Salomon gathered them togither with their legions in a brasen vessell, where were inclosed among all the legions seventie two kings, of whome the cheefe was Bileth, the second was Beliall, the third Asmoday, and above a thousand thousand legions. Without doubt (I must confesse) I learned this of my maister Salomon; but he told me not why he gathered them together, and shut them up so: but I beleeve it was for the pride of this Beliall. Certeine nigromancers doo saie, that Salomon, being on a certeine

42

daie seduced by the craft of a certeine woman, inclined himselfe to praie before the same idoll, Beliall by name: which is not credible. And therefore we must rather thinke (as it is said) that they were gathered together in that great brasen vessell for pride and arrogancie, and throwne into a deepe lake or hole in Babylon. For wise Salomon did accomplish his workes by the divine power, which never forsooke him. And therefore we must thinke he worshipped not the image Beliall; for then he could not have constrained the spirits by divine vertue: for this Beliall, with three kings were in the lake. But the Babylonians woondering at the matter, supposed that they should find therein a great quantitie of treasure, and therefore with one consent went downe into the lake, and uncovered and brake the vessell, out of the which immediatlie flew the capteine divels, and were delivered to their former and proper places. But this Beliall entred into a certeine image, and there gave answer to them that offered and sacrificed unto him: as Tocz. in his sentences reporteth, and the Babylonians did worship and sacrifice thereunto.

(24) Bune is a great and a strong Duke, he appeareth as a dragon with three heads, the third whereof is like to a man; he speaketh with a divine voice, he maketh the dead to change their place, and divels to assemble upon the sepulchers of the dead: he greatlie inricheth a man, and maketh him eloquent and wise, answering trulie to all demands, and thirtie legions obeie him.

(25) Forneus is a great marquesse, like unto a monster of the sea, he maketh men woondeffull in rhetorike, he adorneth a man with a good name, and the knowledge of toongs, and maketh one beloved as well of foes as freends: there are under him nine and twentie legions, of the order partlie of thrones, and partlie of angels.

43

(26) Ronove   Roneve   a marquesse and an earle, he is resembled to a monster, he bringeth singular understanding in rhetorike, faithfull servants, knowledge of toongs, favour of freends and foes; and nineteene legions obeie him.

(27) Berith is a great and a terrible duke, and hath three names. Of some he is called Beall; of the Jewes Berithi Berith ; of Nigromancers Bolfry   Bolfri : he commeth foorth as a red souldier, with red clothing, and upon a horsse of that colour, and a crowne on his head. He answereth trulie of things present, past, and to come. He is compelled at a certeine houre, through divine vertue, by a ring of art magicke. He is also a lier, he turneth all mettals into gold, he adorneth a man with dignities, and confirmeth them, he speaketh with a cleare and a subtill voice, and six and twentie legions are under him.

(28) Astaroth is a great and a strong duke, comming foorth in the shape of a fowle angell, sitting upon an infernall dragon, and carrieng on his right hand a viper: he answereth trulie to matters present, past, and to come, and also of all secrets. He talketh willinglie of the creator of spirits, and of their fall, and how they sinned and fell: he saith he fell not of his owne accord. He maketh a man woonderfull learned in the liberall sciences, he ruleth fourtie legions. Let everie exorcist take heed, that he admit him not too neere him, bicause of his stinking breath lit. "because of the intolerable stench which he exhales" . And therefore let the conjuror hold neere to his face a magicall silver ring, and that shall defend him.

(29) Foras Forras , alias Forcas is a great president, and is seene in the forme of a strong man, and in humane shape, he understandeth the vertue of hearbs and pretious stones: he teacheth fullie logicke, ethicke, and their parts: he maketh a man invisible, wittie, eloquent, and to live long;

he recovereth things lost, and discovereth   discloses
treasures, and is lord over nine and twentie legions.

(30) Furfur is a great earle, appearing as an hart, with a firie
taile, he lieth in everie thing, except he be brought up
within a triangle; being bidden, he taketh angelicall forme,
he speaketh with a hoarse voice, and willinglie maketh love
betweene man and wife or simply "woman" ; he raiseth
thunders and lightnings, and blasts. Where he is
commanded, he answereth well, both of secret and also of
divine things, and hath rule and dominion over six and
twentie legions.

(31) Marchosias Marchocias is a great marquesse, he
sheweth himselfe in the shape of a cruell shee woolfe, with
a griphens wings, with a serpents taile, and spetting I
cannot tell what out of his mouth. When he is in a mans
shape, he is an excellent fighter, he answereth all questions
trulie, he is faithfull in all the conjurors businesse
commands , he was of the order of dominations, under him
are thirtie legions: he hopeth after 1200. yeares to returne to
the seventh throne, but he is deceived in that hope.

(32) Malphas is a great president, he is seene like a crowe,
but being cloathed with humane image, speaketh with a
hoarse voice, be buildeth houses and high towres
wonderfullie, and quicklie bringeth artificers togither, he
throweth downe also the enimies edifications, he helpeth to
good familiars, he receiveth sacrifices willinglie, but he
deceiveth all the sacrificers, there obeie him fourtie legions.

(33) Vepar, alias Separ, a great duke and a strong, he is like
a mermaid, he is the guide of the waters, and of ships laden
with armour; he bringeth to passe (at the commandement of
his master) that the sea shalbe rough and stormie, and shall
appeare full of shippes; he killeth men in three daies, with

putrifieng their wounds, and producing maggots into them; howbeit, they maie be all healed with diligence, he ruleth nine and twentie legions.

(34) Sabnacke Sabnac , alias Salmac, is a great marquesse and a strong, he commeth foorth as an armed soldier with a lions head, sitting on a pale horsse, he dooth marvelouslie change mans forme and favor, he buildeth high towres full of weapons, and also castels and cities; he inflicteth men thirtie daies with wounds both rotten and full of maggots, at the exorcists commandement, he provideth good familiars, and hath dominion over fiftie legions.

(35) Sidonay Sydonay , alias Asmoday, a great king, strong and mightie, he is seene with three heads, whereof the first is like a bull, the second like a man, the third like a ram, he hath a serpents taile, he belcheth flames out of his mouth, he hath feete like a goose, he sitteth on an infernall dragon, he carrieth a lance and a flag in his hand, he goeth before others, which are under the power of Amaymon. When the conjuror exerciseth this office, let him be abroad brave , let him be warie courageous and standing on his feete; if his cap be on his head   ! if he is afraid he will be overwhelmed , he will cause all his dooings to be bewraied divulged , which if he doo not, the exorcist shalbe deceived by Amaymon in everie thing. But so soone as he seeth him in the forme aforesaid, he shall call him by his name, saieng; Thou art Asmoday; he will not denie it, and by and by he boweth downe to the ground; he giveth the ring of venues, he absolutelie teacheth geometrie, arythmetike, astronomie, and handicrafts mechanics . To all demands he answereth fullie and trulie, he maketh a man invisible, he sheweth the places where treasure lieth, and gardeth it, if it be among the legions of Amaymon, he hath under his power seventie two legions.

46

(36) Gaap, alias Tap, a great president and a prince, he appeareth in a meridionall signe, and when he taketh humane shape Clm 849 reads: He appears in the form of a doctor when he takes on a human form. He is the most excellent doctor of women, and he makes them burn with love for men. he is the guide of the foure principall kings, as mightie as Bileth. There were certeine necromancers that offered sacrifices and burnt offerings unto him; and to call him up, they exercised an art, saieng that Salomon the wise made it. Which is false: for it was rather Cham, the sonne of Noah, who after the floud began first to invocate wicked spirits. He invocated Bileth, and made an art in his name, and a booke which is knowne to manie mathematicians. There were burnt offerings and sacrifices made, and gifts given, and much wickednes wrought by the exorcists, who mingled therewithall the holie names of God, the which in that art are everie where expressed. Marie Certainly there is an epistle of those names written by Salomon, as also write Helias Hierosolymitanus and Helisæus. It is to be noted, that if anie exorcist have the art of Bileth, and cannot make him stand before him, nor see him, I may not bewraie how and declare the meanes to conteine him, bicause it is abhomination, and for that I have learned nothing from Salomon of his dignitie and office. But yet I will not hide this; to wit, that he maketh a man woonderfull in philosophie and all the liberall sciences: he maketh love, hatred, insensibilitie, invisibilitie, consecration, and consecration of those things that are belonging unto the domination of Amaymon, and delivereth familiars out of the possession of other conjurors, answering truly and perfectly of things present, past, & to come, & transferreth men most speedilie into other nations, he ruleth sixtie six legions, & was of the order of potestats.

(37) Shax   Chax , alias Scox, is a darke and a great marquesse, like unto a storke, with a hoarse and subtill

47

voice: he dooth marvellouslie take awaie the sight, hearing and understanding of anie man, at the commandement of the conjuror: he taketh awaie monie out of everie kings house, and carrieth it backe after 1200. yeares, if he be commanded, he is a horssestealer, he is thought to be faithfull in all commandements: and although he promise to be obedient to the conjuror in all things; yet is he not so, he is a lier, except he be brought into a triangle, and there he speaketh divinelie, and telleth of things which are hidden, and not kept of wicked spirits, he promiseth good familiars, which are accepted if they be not deceivers, he hath thirtie legions.

(38) Procell is a great and a strong duke, appearing in the shape of an angell, but speaketh verie darklie of things hidden, he teacheth geometrie and all the liberall arts, he maketh great noises, and causeth the waters to rore, where are none, he warmeth waters, and distempereth bathes at certeine times, as the exorcist appointeth him, he was of the order of potestats, and hath fourtie eight legions under his power.

(39) Furcas is a knight and commeth foorth in the similitude of a cruell man, with a long beard and a hoarie head, he sitteth on a pale horsse, carrieng in his hand a sharpe weapon dart or spear , he perfectlie teacheth practike philosophie, rhetorike, logike, astronomie, chiromancie, pyromancie, and their parts: there obeie him twentie legions.

(40) Murmur is a great duke and an earle, appearing in the shape of a souldier, riding on a griphen vulture , with a dukes crowne on his head; there go before him two of his ministers, with great trumpets, he teacheth philosophie absolutelie, he constraineth soules to come before the

exorcist, to answer what he shall aske them, he was of the order partlie of thrones, and partlie of angels, and ruleth thirtie legions.

(41) Caim Caym is a great president, taking the forme of a thrush blackbird , but when he putteth on man's shape, he answereth in burning ashes, carrieng in his hand a most sharpe swoord, he maketh the best disputers, he giveth men the understanding of all birds, of the lowing of bullocks, and barking of dogs, and also of the sound and noise of waters, he answereth best of things to come, he was of the order of angels, and ruleth thirtie legions of divels.

(42) Raum, or Raim is a great earle, he is seene as a crowe, but when he putteth on humane shape, at the commandement of the exorcist, he stealeth woonderfullie out of the kings house, and carrieth it whether he is assigned, he destroieth cities, and hath great despite unto dignities, he knoweth things present, past, and to come, and reconcileth freends and foes, he was of the order of thrones, and governeth thirtie legions.

(43) Halphas is a great earle, and commeth abroad like a storke, with a hoarse voice, he notablie buildeth up townes full of munition and weapons, he sendeth men of warre to places appointed, and hath under him six and twentie legions.

(44) Focalor is a great duke comming foorth as a man, with wings like a griphen, he killeth men, and drowneth them in the waters, and overturneth ships of warre, commanding and ruling both winds and seas. And let the conjuror note, that if he bid him hurt no man, he willinglie consenteth thereto: he hopeth after 1000. yeares to returne to the seventh throne, but he is deceived, he hath three legions.

(45) Vine is a great king and an earle, he showeth himselfe as a lion, riding on a blacke horsse, and carrieth a viper in his hand, he gladlie buildeth large towres, he throweth downe stone walles, and maketh waters rough. At the commandement of the exorcist he answereth of things hidden, of witches, and of things present, past, and to come.

(46) Bifrons is seene in the similitude of a monster, when he taketh the image of a man, he maketh one woonderfull cunning in astrologie, absolutelie declaring the mansions of the planets, he dooth the like in geometrie, and other admesurements, he perfectlie understandeth the strength and vertue of hearbs, pretious stones, and woods, he changeth dead bodies from place to place, he seemeth to light candles upon the sepulchres of the dead, and hath under him six and twentie legions.

(47) Gamigin Gamygyn is a great marquesse, and is seene in the forme of a little horsse, when he taketh humane shape he speaketh with a hoarse voice, disputing of all liberall sciences; he bringeth also to passe, that the soules, which are drowned in the sea, or which dwell in purgatorie (which is called Cartagra, that is, affliction of soules) shall take aierie bodies, and evidentlie appeare and answer to interrogatories at the conjurors commandement; he tarrieth with the exorcist, untill he have accomplished his desire, and hath thirtie legions under him.

(48) Zagan Zagam is a great king and a president, he commeth abroad like a bull, with griphens wings, but when he taketh humane shape, he maketh men wittie, he turneth all mettals into the coine of that dominion, and turneth water into wine, and wine into water, he also turneth bloud into wine oil , & wine oil into bloud, & a foole into a wise man, he is head of thirtie and three legions.

(49) Orias is a great marquesse, and is seene as a lion riding on a strong horsse, with a serpents taile, and carrieth in his right hand two great serpents hissing, he knoweth the mansion of planets and perfectlie teacheth the vertues of the starres, he transformeth men, he giveth dignities, prelacies, and confirmations, and also the favour of freends and foes, and hath under him thirtie legions.

(50) Valac   Volac   is a great president, and commeth abroad with angels wings like a boie, riding on a twoheaded dragon, he perfectlie answereth of treasure hidden, and where serpents may be seene, which he delivereth into the conjurors hands, void of anie force or strength, and hath dominion over thirtie legions of divels.

(51) Gomory a strong and a mightie duke, he appeareth like a faire woman, with a duchesse crownet about hir midle, riding on a camell, he answereth well and truelie of things present, past, and to come, and of treasure hid, and where it lieth: he procureth the love of women, especiallie of maids, and hath six and twentie legions.

(52) Decarabia or Carabia, he commeth like a * and knoweth the force of herbes and pretious stones, and maketh all birds flie before the exorcist, and to tarrie with him, as though they were tame, and that they shall drinke and sing, as their maner is, and hath thirtie legions.

(53) Amduscias a great and a strong duke, he commeth foorth as an unicorne, when he standeth before his maister in humane shape, being commanded, he easilie bringeth to passe, that trumpets and all musicall instruments may be heard and not seene, and also that trees shall bend and incline, according to the conjurors will, he is excellent among familiars, and hath nine and twentie legions.

(54) Andras is a great marquesse, and is seene in an angels shape with a head like a blacke night raven, riding upon a blacke and a verie strong woolfe, flourishing with a sharpe sword in his hand, he can kill the maister, the servant, and all assistants, he is author of discords, and ruleth thirtie legions.

(55) Andrealphus Androalphus is a great marquesse, appearing as a pecocke, he raiseth great noises, and in humane shape perfectlie teacheth geometrie, and all things belonging to admeasurements, he maketh a man to be a subtill disputer, and cunning in astronomie, and transformeth a man into the likenes of a bird, and there are under him thirtie legions.

(56) Ose Oze is a great president, and commeth foorth like a leopard, and counterfeting to be a man, he maketh one cunning in the liberall sciences, he answereth truelie of divine and secret things, he transformeth a mans shape, and bringeth a man to that madnes or, "drives insanity away" , that he thinketh himselfe to be that which he is not; as that he is a king or a pope, or that he weareth a crowne on his head, Durátque id regnum ad horam and makes the kingdom of time endure.

(57) Aym or Haborim Haborym is a great duke and a strong, he commeth foorth with three heads, the first like a serpent, the second like a man having two * the third like a cat, he rideth on a viper, carrieng in his hand a light fier brand, with the flame whereof castels and cities are fiered, he maketh one wittie everie kind of waie, he answereth truelie of privie matters, and reigneth over twentie six legions.

(58) Orobas is a great prince, he commeth foorth like a horsse, but when he putteth on him a mans idol image , he

talketh of divine vertue, he giveth true answers of things present, past, and to come, and of the divinitie, and of the creation, he deceiveth none, nor suffereth anie to be tempted, he giveth dignities and prelacies, and the favour of freends and foes, and hath rule over twentie legions.

(59) Vapula is a great duke and a strong, he is seene like a lion with griphens wings, he maketh a man subtill and wonderfull in handicrafts mechanics , philosophie, and in sciences conteined in bookes, and is ruler over thirtie six legions.

(60) Cimeries is a great marquesse and a strong, ruling in the parts of Aphrica Africa ; he teacheth perfectlie grammar, logicke, and rhetorike, he discovereth treasures and things hidden, he bringeth to passe, that a man shall seeme with expedition to be turned into a soldier, he rideth upon a great blacke horsse, and ruleth twentie legions.

(61) Amy is a great president, and appeareth in a flame of fier, but having taken mans shape, he maketh one marvelous in astrologie, and in all the liberall sciences, he procureth excellent familiars, he bewraieth treasures preserved by spirits, he hath the governement of thirtie six legions, he is partlie of the order of angels, partlie of potestats, he hopeth after a thousand two hundreth yeares to returne to the seventh throne: which is not credible.

(62) Flauros a strong duke, is seene in the forme of a terrible strong leopard, in humane shape, he sheweth a terrible countenance, and fierie eies, he answereth trulie and fullie of things present, past, and to come; if he be in a triangle, he lieth in all things and deceiveth in other things, and beguileth in other busines, he gladlie talketh of the divinitie, and of the creation of the world, and of the fall; he is constrained by divine vertue, and so are all divels or

spirits, to burne and destroie all the conjurors adversaries. And if he be commanded, he suffereth the conjuror not to be tempted, and he hath twentie legions under him.

(63) Balam is a great and a terrible king, he commeth foorth with three heads, the first of a bull, the second of a man, the third of a ram, he hath a serpents taile, and flaming eies, riding upon a furious very powerful beare, and carrieng a hawke on his fist, he speaketh with a hoarse voice, answering perfectlie of things present, past, and to come, hee maketh a man invisible and wise, hee governeth fourtie legions, and was of the order of dominations.

(64) Allocer Alocer is a strong duke and a great, he commeth foorth like a soldier, riding on a great horsse, he hath a lions face, verie red, and with flaming eies, he speaketh with a big voice, he maketh a man woonderfull in astronomie, and in all the liberall sciences, he bringeth good familiars, and ruleth thirtie six legions.

(65) Saleos Zaleos is a great earle, he appeareth as a gallant handsome soldier, riding on a crocodile, and weareth a dukes crowne, peaceable, &c.

(66) Vuall Wal is a great duke and a strong, he is seene as a great and terrible dromedarie, but in humane forme, he soundeth out in a base deep voice the Ægyptian toong. This man above all other procureth the especiall love of women, and knoweth things present, past, and to come, procuring the love of freends and foes, he was of the order of potestats, and governeth thirtie seven legions.

(67) Haagenti is a great president, appearing like a great bull, having the wings of a griphen, but when he taketh humane shape, he maketh a man wise in everie thing, he changeth all mettals into gold, and changeth wine and water

the one into the other, and commandeth as manie legions as Zagan.

(68) Phoenix is a great marquesse, appearing like the bird Phoenix, having a childs voice: but before he standeth still before the conjuror, he singeth manie sweet notes. Then the exorcist with his companions must beware he give no eare to the melodie, but must by and by bid him put on humane shape; then will he speake marvellouslie of all woonderfull sciences. He is an excellent poet, and obedient, he hopeth to returne to the seventh throne after a thousand two hundreth yeares, and governeth twentie legions.

(69) Stolas is a great prince, appearing in the forme of a nightraven, before the exorcist, he taketh the image and shape of a man, and teacheth astronomie, absolutelie understanding the vertues of herbes and pretious stones; there are under him twentie six legions.

 Note that a legion is 6 6 6 6, and now by multiplication count how manie legions doo arise out of everie particular.

This was the work of one T. R. written in faire letters of red & blacke upõ parchment, and made by him, Ann. 1570. to the maintenance of his living, the edifieng of the poore, and the glorie of gods holie name: as he himselfe saith.

The secret of secrets; Thou that workst them, be secret in them.

CHAPTER III.

The houres wherin principall divels may be bound, to wit, raised and restrained from dooing of hurt.

AMAYMON king of the east, Gorson king of the south, Zimimar king of the north, Goap king and prince of the west, may be bound from the third houre, till noone, and from the ninth houre till evening.

Marquesses may be bound from the ninth houre till compline, and from compline till the end of the daie.

Dukes may be hound from the first houre till noone; and cleare wether is to be observed.

Prelates may be bound in anie houre of the daie.

Knights from daie dawning, till sunne rising; or from evensong, till the sunne set.

A President may not be bound in anie houre of the daie, except the king, whome he obeieth, be invocated; nor in the shutting of the evening.

Counties or erles may be bound at anie houre of the daie, so it be in the woods or feelds, where men resort not.

CHAPTER IV.

The forme of adjuring or citing of the spirits aforesaid to arise and appeare.

WHEN you will have anie spirit,you must know his name and office; you must also fast, and be cleane from all pollution, three or foure daies before; so will the spirit be the more obedient unto you. Then make a circle, and call up the spirit with great intention,and holding a ring in your hand, rehearse in your owne name, and your companions (for one must alwaies be with you) this praier following, and so no spirit shall annoie you, and your purpose shall take effect.   (And note how this agreeth with popish charmes and conjurations.)

In the name of our Lord Jesus Christ the ✟ father ✟ and the sonne ✟ and the Hollie-ghost ✟ holie trinitie and unseparable unitie, I call upon thee, that thou maiest be my salvation and defense, and the protection of my bodie and soule, and of all my goods through the vertue of thy holie crosse, and through the vertue of thy passion, I beseech thee O Lord Jesus Christ, by the merits of thy blessed mother S. Marie, and of all thy saints, that thou give me grace and divine power over all the wicked spirits, so as which of them soever I doo call by name, they may come by and by from everie coast, and accomplish my will, that they neither be hurtfull or fearefull unto me, but rather obedient and diligent about me. And through thy vertue streightlie commanding them, let them fulfill my commandements, Amen. Holie, holie, Lord God of sabboth, which wilt come to judge the quicke and the dead, thou which art A and Omega, first and last, King of kings and Lord of lords, Ioth, Aglanabrath, El, Abiel, Anathiel anathi Enathiel , Amazim, Sedomel, Gayes, Tolima, Elias, Ischiros, Athanatos, Ymas Heli, Messias, Tolimi, Elias, Ischiros, Athanatos, Imas . By these thy holie names, and by all other I doo call upon thee, and beseech thee O Lord Jesus Christ, by thy nativitie and baptisme, by thy crosse and passion, by thine ascension, and by the comming of the Holie-ghost, by the bitternesse of thy soule when it departed from thy bodie, by thy five wounds, by the bloud and water which went out of thy bodie, by thy vertue, by the sacrament which thou gavest thy disciples the daie before thou sufferedst, by the holie trinitie, and by the inseparable unitie, by blessed Marie thy mother, by thine angels, archangels, prophets, patriarchs, and by all thy saints, and by all the sacraments which are made in thine honour, I doo worship and beseech thee, I blesse and desire thee, to accept these prayers, conjurations, and words of my mouth, which I will use. I require thee O Lord Jesus Christ, that thou give me thy vertue & power over all thine angels (which were throwne downe from heaven to deceive mankind) to drawe them to me, to tie and bind them, & also to loose them, to gather them togither before me, & to command them to doo all that they can, and that by no meanes they contemne my voice, or the words of my mouth; but that they obeie me and my saiengs, and feare me. I beseech thee by thine humanitie, mercie and grace, and I require thee Adonay, Amay, Horta, Vege dora, Mitai, Hel, Suranat, Ysion, Ysesy, and by all thy holie names, and by all thine holie he saints and she saints, by all thine angels and archangels, powers, dominations, and vertues, and by that name that Salomon did bind the divels, and shut them up, Elhrach, Ebanher, Agle, Goth, Ioth, Othie, Venoch, Nabrat, and by all thine holie names which are written in this booke, and by the vertue of them all, that thou enable me to congregate all thy spirits throwne downe from heaven, that they may give me a true answer of all my demands, and that they satisfie all my requests, without the hurt of my bodie or soule, or any thing else that is mine, through our Lord Jesus Christ thy sonne, which liveth and reigneth with thee in the unitie of the Holie-ghost, one God world without end.

Oh father omnipotent, oh wise sonne, oh Holie-ghost, the searcher of harts, oh you three in persons, one true godhead in substance, which didst spare Adam and Eve in their sins; and oh thou sonne, which diedst for their sinnes a most filthie disgraceful death, susteining it upon the holie crosse; oh thou most mercifull, when I flie unto thy mercie, and beseech thee by all the means I can, by these the holie names of thy sonne; to wit, A and Omega, and all other his names, grant me thy vertue and power, that I may be able to cite before me, thy spirits which were throwne downe from heaven, & that they may speake with me, & dispatch by & by without delaie, & with a good will, & without the hurt of my bodie, soule, or goods, &c: as is conteined in the booke called Annulus Salomonis.

Oh great and eternall vertue of the highest, which through disposition, these being called to judgement, Vaicheon, Stimulamaton, Esphares,Tetragrammaton, Olioram, Cryon irion , Esytion, Existion, Eriona, Onela, Brasim, Noym, Messias, Soter, Emanuel, Sabboth Sabaoth , Adonay, I worship thee, I invocate thee, I imploie thee with all the strength of my mind, that by thee, my present praiers, consecrations, and conjurations be hallowed: and whersoever wicked spirits are called, in the vertue of thy names, they may come togither from everie coast, and diligentlie fulfill the will of me the exorcist. Fiat, fiat, fiat, Amen.

(5) This kind of blasphemy and swearing constitutes the worst kind of refuse and dregs of the earth, and punishment of these profane magi is well deserved.

END

www.ingramcontent.com/pod-product-compliance
Lightning Source LLC
Chambersburg PA
CBHW071750090426
42738CB00011B/2631